Rabbits and Hares

Rabbits and Hares

Ralph Whitlock

Priory Press Limited

Young Naturalist Books

Squirrels

Foxes

Bats

Rabbits and Hares

Hedgehogs

Frogs and Toads

Snakes and Lizards

Badgers

Deer

Spiders

Otters

Rats and Mice

SBN 85078 182 5
Copyright © 1974 Priory Press Ltd
First published in 1974 by
Priory Press Ltd
101 Grays Inn Rd, London WC1

Filmset by Keyspools Ltd, Golborne, Lancs.
Printed in Great Britain by
The Pitman Press, Bath.

Contents

1 : Which are Rabbits and Which are Hares?

To look at, rabbits and hares are very like each other. Both have long ears, big eyes and short, white, tufty tails which show up when they are running away. Both live by eating plants. Both can run very fast.

Their habits, however, are very different. Hares live alone in open fields. Rabbits are gregarious, which means that they like crowding together. They dig a maze of underground tunnels, in which lots of them live.

When a hare sleeps it does so squatting in a shallow depression in the soil or under a tuft of grass. This it makes by stamping its feet and turning round and round. The depression is called a *form* and it is always in a place from which the hare can see any danger approaching from any direction. When a rabbit sleeps it does so in the darkness of its burrow, underground.

A female hare deposits her newborn young in a form, one baby to each form. The young hares, which are known as *leverets*, are born with their eyes open and with a full coat of golden-brown fur. These lovely little creatures can run about when they are a few hours old.

Left : A brown hare sits in the snow.

An American cottontail rabbit.

8

A brown hare crouches in a field. With its bulging eyes it can see sideways and backwards as well as forwards.

A female rabbit also goes off on her own when her young are about to be born, but she needs to make much more careful preparation for her family. She digs or finds a short burrow, at the end of which she enlarges the tunnel to form a nest. She lines it with dry, soft grasses and with her own fur, plucked from her stomach.

The young, which may be as many as six or eight in a litter, are born blind and naked. They are ten days old before they open their eyes. They get their fur coat by

9

A young blue hare. Blue hares do not live quite so much on their own as brown hares do.

about the same time. When the mother rabbit leaves her nesting burrow she always conceals the entrance by scooping earth, leaves or grasses over it. She has to burrow her way in every time she returns to feed her babies. The *stop*, as the nesting burrow is called, is only

left open when the young are ready to emerge from the

A nestful of baby cottontails. Hares are born furry, rabbits naked.

nest to take their first look at the outside world. This happens when they are about a month old.

Rabbits and hares are found in most countries of the world. Britain has one kind of rabbit and two of hares. They are the Brown Hare and the Alpine Hare. Ireland has a hare of its own, the Irish Hare. America has several more kinds of hares and several rabbits. It is rather confusing that one kind of hare, the commonest, is known in America as the Jack Rabbit. It is a real hare, though. It has much the same habits as the brown hare. The commonest American rabbit is known as the Cottontail Rabbit, or just the Cottontail.

A black-tailed jack rabbit resting on the plains of Texas. In Britain it would be called a hare, not a rabbit.

2: The Habits of the Brown Hare

The Brown Hare, which is the common one in Britain, is about 24 inches long and weighs about 8 pounds. Its white tail is three or four inches long. Generally the male is rather smaller than the female.

The brown hare is golden-brown, or tawny, like a lion, with some dark brown markings. It blends very well with the dry grasses or ploughed fields where the hare squats. The underparts are white. The white tail is black on top, but you do not often see this side of it as it is usually laid flat against the hare's back. The very long, large ears have black tips. Because the hare is outdoors in all weathers, its fur is long, with a warm, soft undercoat. The hare also has many long whiskers, which are almost always twitching.

Hares moult, or shed their coats, twice a year—once in autumn and once in spring.

A peculiar feature of the hare is its cleft upper lip. It is split, from nose to teeth. Children born with a similar deformity are said to have a "hare lip."

Old books on natural history used to repeat the old country belief that some hares grow horns. It is not true.

Above: A brown hare hurries to the side of a field, showing its black and white tail.
Right: Looking around to make sure no enemies are approaching.

The Habits of the Brown Hare

Hares are very strong animals, and much of their strength lies in their long, powerful hind legs, which are something like a kangaroo's. When a hare moves about the countryside it usually progresses by a series of leaps rather than by running. A hare can keep up a speed of 30 to 40 miles an hour quite easily, though generally it prefers to dodge rather than keep a straight course. It can run for long distances. It can also jump over high fences or hedges and over streams. If it wishes, it can swim quite well. In fact, hares seem to like water and often bathe for fun.

A hare sits up on a lonely forest path.

Hares can run as fast as 40 m.p.h., in great leaps and bounds.

Another remarkable feature of the hare is its large, bulging eyes. They are set in the sides of its head, so that the hare, sitting in its form, can see behind it and on all sides as well as in front. It can in fact see things rather more easily when they are on one side than when they are in front of it. When chased by dogs it tends to run in a very large circle, so that it can see the hounds all the time.

17

Above : March hares gather in a field to celebrate the coming of the mating season.
Right : Jack hares excitedly chase each other round.

In *Alice in Wonderland* we read about the Mad Hatter and the March Hare. Mad March hares were known long before Lewis Carroll wrote about this one. In early spring male hares, which are known as jack hares, assemble in groups in fields and behave quite crazily. They chase each other around in small circles. They stand up on their hind legs and box with each other. They leap high into the air, kicking out at each other with their long hind legs. Some-times they manage to score a kick on another hare,

Romping March hares.

Sometimes the hares get so excited that there is a stand-up boxing match.

making the fur fly. They do all this through excitement, because spring is just arriving and it is time for mating. Often they will travel for long distances to take part in these strange meetings.

The females also sometimes attend and occasionally join in the sparring. Each female has her own territory, or area of countryside which she regards as her own property. Within its limits she finds most of her food, and within it she deposits, at specially chosen spots, her babies. She returns to each baby at some time during the day or night, to feed it. For the rest of the time the little hare sits perfectly still, its golden brown colour blending with the dry grass which surrounds it. Its camouflage is perfect. By the time it is one month old the young hare is able to look after itself.

The baby hare thus becomes independent much earlier than the baby rabbit. Throughout its life the hare is an independent, solitary animal. Apart from the spring meetings, each hare usually avoids other hares. It never digs burrows, though occasionally hares have been known to enter the burrows of other animals.

Although the mating antics of mad March hares usually occur only in spring, female hares can produce young at all seasons of the year. Generally they have at least three litters of youngsters each year, and sometimes they have four. The gestation period, or time between mating and the birth of the young, is between forty and forty-five days.

Female hares are known as *does*. It is said that they will call their young with a very shrill, high-pitched note. Perhaps the young answer, with a note that human beings cannot hear, and this may be how the doe finds the leverets in a field on a dark night.

At other times hares utter a kind of grunt or bleat. When they are hurt or frightened they scream, like a child in pain.

A three-week-old leveret crouches among some rocks. Hares spend their early lives lying silently still, hoping not to be noticed.

3: The Brown Hare's Food

Hares are vegetarian, which means that they eat plants and nothing else. The plants, however, can be of almost any kind, including grasses, roots, vegetables, mushrooms and the bark of trees. It is said that hares do not drink, but that is probably not true. Most likely damp vegetation, moistened by night dew, provides all the water they need. People who have kept tame hares have found that they willingly drink milk. As a rule, hares are nocturnal feeders. They come out to feed in the evenings, and spend most of the day crouched in their forms.

Hares have one strange habit which we find unpleasant and repulsive. They eat their own dung.

The process is, in fact, not quite as unusual as it seems. It is very similar to what happens with cows. When a cow finds itself in a field of luscious grass it eats as much as it possibly can, without bothering to digest it properly. Later, when it has leisure, it sits down, brings back the grass from its stomach and chews it again. This is called "chewing the cud." We can see cows doing it on any farm which has cattle. A hare also swallows much of its

A young leveret is small enough to fit into a man's hand.

food in a hurry. Instead of returning it from the stomach to the mouth, like the cow does, it passes the food right through its body and then eats the pellets. Once it has digested the food this second time round, however, it never swallows the second lot of pellets.

26

A leveret huddles in its form in the long grass of an open field.

Because of this habit, which is known as *refection*, some nations regard hares as unclean animals and will not eat their flesh.

Living as they do on farmland, hares do much damage to farmers' crops. In particular they eat large quantities of young corn in spring and roots in autumn and winter. They also nibble the tops of young forest trees and the bark of big ones, and so are not liked by foresters.

Apart from man, adult hares have few enemies in Britain as most large flesh-eating animals have been killed off. Foxes, stoats and birds of prey catch and eat young hares, when they can find them, which is why the young hares stay perfectly still in their forms.

Left: A young hare nibbles at a thistle.
Below: An unusual sight. A hawk has attacked and killed a full-sized hare larger than itself.

4: Hares in Northern Countries

The Irish Hare is very like the brown hare of Britain but is rather smaller and has longer ears. In Northern Ireland some hares turn white or partly white in winter.

The other British hare is the Alpine Hare, which is found in Scotland. It is also known as the Blue Hare, or Variable Hare. Its fur is not bright blue but a bluish grey. It is much smaller than the brown hare, being about twenty inches long and weighing five or six pounds. Its ears are much shorter, too, but have black tips.

In winter most Alpine hares turn white, to match the snow which covers the mountains where they live. It is extremely difficult to see an Alpine hare when it is crouching in the snow in winter. The tips of its ears always remain black, however, in winter as in summer, and the hair on the soles of its feet is always brown.

As well as making a form in the heather, the Alpine hare sometimes takes refuge in little caves and under great stones. Unlike the brown hare, it sometimes digs short burrows, both to hide in and also to put its young in when they are small.

Left : The Blue or Variable Hare.

32 />

32

Two blue hares crouch watchfully in a field.

In summer the Arctic hare is brown; in the winter it turns white so that it cannot be seen in the snow.

Brown hares are found throughout Europe, except in the far north. Alpine hares live on mountains and in the Arctic regions of Europe and Asia. In America other varieties of Arctic hare take over. Most of the American Arctic hares are larger even than the brown hare and much larger than the European Alpine hare. They are thirty inches long and weigh ten or eleven pounds. Arctic hares change into pure white coats in winter and have very powerful paws, to enable them to dig in the snow for their food.

5: Hares in America and Elsewhere

Besides the Arctic hare, several other kinds of hare are found in America, but the Americans call them all rabbits. There is the Jack Rabbit, of which there are several varieties. The jack rabbit is very similar to the brown hare, but its coat is rather greyer. One variety of jack rabbit has a tail that is all white; another has a tail white on the underside and black on top.

Jack rabbits, like brown hares, live on grassy plains and on farms; also in semi-desert country. They are sometimes very numerous. Years ago one small county in the state of Oregon offered a grant for every jack rabbit killed, and in one year it paid out on over a million animals. It is said that jack rabbits get their name from their long ears, which reminded early settlers in America of the long ears of a donkey, or jack ass.

Another American hare, much smaller than the jack rabbit and very like the Alpine hare in appearance, is the Snowshoe Rabbit, or Varying Hare. It is about sixteen inches long and weighs from three to five pounds. It gets its name *Snowshoe* from the pads of hair on the soles of its

Above : A Snowshoe rabbit, well camouflaged in the snow.
Left : The long ears of an American jack rabbit.
Below : An antelope jack rabbit, so called because of its long, skinny legs.

feet, which enable it to run over snow in winter. As with many other northern animals, its coat turns white in winter. It is a forest animal, living mostly on the twigs and bark of trees.

In spite of the confusing names, the distinction between hares and rabbits, explained earlier, applies to America as well as to Europe. Hares are born with a coat of fur and with their eyes open. Rabbits are born naked and with their eyes closed. So all the animals mentioned so far in this chapter are hares.

On the American continent during the short northern

The Snowshoe Rabbit or Varying Hare has, like the Alpine Hare, shorter darker ears and long, padded feet.

summer the countryside, right up to the Arctic Ocean, is covered with a carpet of small flowering plants, as well as with mosses and lichens. This provides food for many kinds of grazing animals, including hares, which from time to time become extremely numerous. Some of the northern hares have as many as five litters of young in a season, each litter with three or four babies. As the numbers of hares increase, so do the numbers of the animals which prey on them. Foxes, stoats, minks, owls, eagles and, above all, lynxes join in this population explosion. Then, for some unknown reason, the population

And like the Alpine hare its coat turns brown in summer to match the moss and lichen around it.

A snowshoe rabbit sits stock still, hoping not to be noticed in the snow and shadows.

crashes, and for several years both hares and the animals which eat them become quite scarce, until the cycle starts all over again.

Another curious thing about hares is that the ones which live in the north have shorter ears than those in southern climates. Large ears are, of course, necessary for animals like hares, which have many natural enemies and rely on their ears as well as on their eyes and noses to tell them when danger is approaching. But it is a law of nature that the larger the surface an animal exposes to the weather the more quickly it loses heat. In the tropics, therefore, it is an advantage for hares to have large ears. Some of the African desert hares have very large ears indeed, and these help them to sit all day long in a form in desert country without becoming uncomfortably hot. In the Arctic, however, hares need to retain their body heat, not to lose it, and so they have short ears. The ears of the Arctic hare are stumpy, and shorter than a rabbit's.

Pampas hares of South America have much shorter ears than their northern cousins.

There are several kinds of hare in Africa. Most of them are very similar to the European and American hares, though the Red Rock Hares of South Africa have big, bushy tails. In India the Black-necked Hare has started to come into villages, looking for food on rubbish dumps.

Africa also has several Jumping Hares or Spring Hares, but these are not really hares but are rodents, related to the Dormouse.

A long-legged African hare from Kenya.

6: Hares and Man

The flesh of most hares is good to eat. It is generally boiled, stewed or cooked in a pot with vegetables, or baked in a pie, and is served with redcurrant jelly. It is a rather dark reddish brown in colour.

Hares are therefore often killed for food, as well as because they are a nuisance to farmers and foresters.

They are caught and killed in a number of ways. In the old days they were often driven by hounds into nets and killed there. Owing to their habit of following well marked tracks, or *runs*, every day (or night), it is also easy to catch them by snares set in these tracks. They are also shot, usually in organized hare "drives" in winter.

Four sorts of dog, or hound, are used to chase hares. Hunting hares by greyhounds is known as *coursing*. Hares are also hunted by packs of beagles, which are hounds with rather short legs; by harriers, which are like foxhounds but much smaller; and by basset hounds, which are larger and heavier than harriers but have very short legs. All these methods of hunting hares are regarded as sport. Beagles are usually followed by men on foot; harriers usually by horsemen. Basset hounds are not much used nowadays. Harriers, beagles and bassets hunt by scent, greyhounds by sight.

Hundreds of years ago, hares were thought to be witches' animals. It was said that witches could turn themselves into hares. Like cats, a hare is sometimes referred to as "Puss."

In recent years a curious reaction by hares to a human invention has been noticed. Hares have developed a remarkable liking for airfields. They often assemble there

A hare's powerful leap takes him well clear of the stream he is jumping.

A snowshoe vanishes over the stump of a tree.

in large numbers, at times other than the mating season. It may be because they like the open grassland where they can lie or graze without fear of interference, but it seems also that they enjoy the noise and vibration of aircraft. Hares react to thunder by stamping or drumming on the ground with their feet, and perhaps the noise of planes landing and taking off reminds them of thunder.

Outside the mating season it is unusual to find two Brown hares together.

7: Rabbits and their Food

Rabbits are much smaller than brown hares. They weigh from three to five pounds and are about eighteen inches long. In colour they are much greyer than hares, with greyish white underparts. Their ears are short (about half as long as the brown hare's) and have no black tips. Like hares, they have split upper lips and many whiskers. Their hind legs are shorter, though very strong. Their short tail is white underneath and is generally carried curved upwards over the back. When the rabbit is running away, its white tail is very conspicuous and serves as a warning to other rabbits. This also happens with hares.

Rabbits, like hares, live on grassland and farms but also in woods. Whereas hares escape from their enemies by running very fast and for long distances, rabbits hide underground. A rabbit can run at a high speed for a short distance but soon tires.

Rabbits are gregarious, which means that they like each other's company and live together in colonies. The underground burrows which they dig are connected with each other to form a maze of tunnels. This maze is called

48 *Above and right :* The common European rabbit. Their numbers increase rapidly—and they never seem to stop eating!

a *warren*. Here many rabbits, sometimes a hundred or more, make their home.

Rabbits do not usually line their underground burrows with grass or anything else but sit on the bare earth. They usually come out to feed at night, though sometimes,

Wild rabbits drinking at a water hole in South Australia. When there was nothing to control their numbers, they multiplied enormously.

when they think it is safe, they venture out by day as well, and they like sunning themselves outside their burrows.

They will eat most vegetation and have large appetites. A rabbit will eat 180 grammes of grass a day. They particularly like farm crops, such as wheat, oats, barley,

Coming out at dusk for a drink.

roots and vegetables, as well as grass, and do immense damage. In winter they eat the bark and shoots of trees and will sometimes kill many trees by "ring-barking", which means gnawing off a circle of bark right around a tree trunk, so that the sap cannot rise.

Rabbits, like hares, have the habit of refection (see page 25).

Although rabbits are not adapted for climbing, they will occasionally climb trees that offer an easy foothold and will sometimes lie up in hollow trees. They can also swim.

When they need to be, rabbits can be strong swimmers.

8 : How Rabbits Breed

Rabbits are *polygamous*, which means that each male, or buck, mates with a number of does. Each doe has her own territory, which is an area of land not far from the central warren. Often when she has finished with her nesting burrow, which is made on this territory, it is extended to join up with the warren, and so the colony is always growing.

The nesting burrow, which the doe herself digs, is a rather short one, three or four feet long, and, unlike the burrows of the main warren, ends in a kind of little room which is lined with hay, straw or some other soft and dry vegetation. A day or two before the young are born the doe adds another lining of fur, plucked from her body.

Here the young are born, blind and naked, thirty or forty days after mating has occurred. The mother rabbit does not stay with them all the time but goes out to find her food, returning to feed her family two or three times in a day and night. When she leaves her nesting burrow, or *stop*, she carefully covers it with earth and refuse, so that no enemy can find it.

Baby rabbits in their nest. Their mother plucks fur from her stomach to line the nest and keep them warm. The young are born naked and blind.

The number of young rabbits per litter can be anything from two to seven or eight. Their eyes open at ten days old, and the young are weaned when they are about a month old. Another litter is often born five or six weeks after the first one. Although many young rabbits die or are killed, each doe rabbit produces, on average, ten or eleven live young ones each year.

Rabbits become adult at the age of three or four months, so rabbits born in spring are quite capable of producing families of their own by autumn. The main breeding season is from January to June (in Britain), but young rabbits can be seen in every season of the year. Because of the high breeding rate, the rabbit population can increase very quickly.

Rabbits are not usually aggressive animals. They would rather run away than fight. That is why we sometimes call

Young rabbits take one of their first breaths of fresh air at the mouth of their burrow.

a timid person a rabbit. The males, however, often fight among themselves, and an old buck will drive away younger males. Does, too, will fight with each other. In particular, a doe will chase away another doe who trespasses on the territory where her nesting burrow is. A doe will also fight any animal which threatens her young. She will attack stoats, weasels and even dogs. A rabbit can be quite a formidable fighter. It scratches with its long front nails and can give dangerous kicks with its powerful hind legs. People who do not know how to handle even a tame rabbit often have their arms and hands gashed with long, festering scratches from the rabbit's hind legs.

9: Where Did Rabbits Come From?

Rabbits are not natives of Britain. There are no records of them for Roman or Saxon times, nor have their bones been found in kitchen waste, dug up by archaeologists, for those remote centuries. It seems that the Normans brought them over from France, partly for food and partly for sport, in the twelfth or thirteenth centuries. Before they came to France they lived in Spain, which is their native country. It is said that the name *Spain* is derived from *tsapan*, the Phoenician word for a rabbit. So Spain was thought of as the land of rabbits.

At first, rabbits were very scarce and expensive in England. The warrens in which they lived were specially made for them and were carefully protected. On maps of the English countryside we can find many farms known as Warren Farm. These were farms near an old rabbit warren. Even after rabbits had lived in England for three hundred years they had not become very common, for it is recorded that in the year 1607 two rabbits cost as much as twelve hens or over fifty dozen eggs.

Later they became very numerous and a pest to farmers.

An enquiry made in 1948 showed that more than 7,000,000 rabbit carcases were despatched by rail from stations in England and Wales. Many more were eaten where they were killed, and many others were sent to market by road. So the number killed that year must have been at least double, or over 14,000,000. Yet rabbits remained as plentiful as ever.

The word *rabbit*, by the way, was at first used only for the young, or as a pet name, much as we used the word *bunny*. Adult rabbits were known as *coneys*, and English

A rabbit hurtles through the air. Rabbits cannot run as fast as hares, but they are hard to catch because they dodge and zigzag to escape their pursuers.

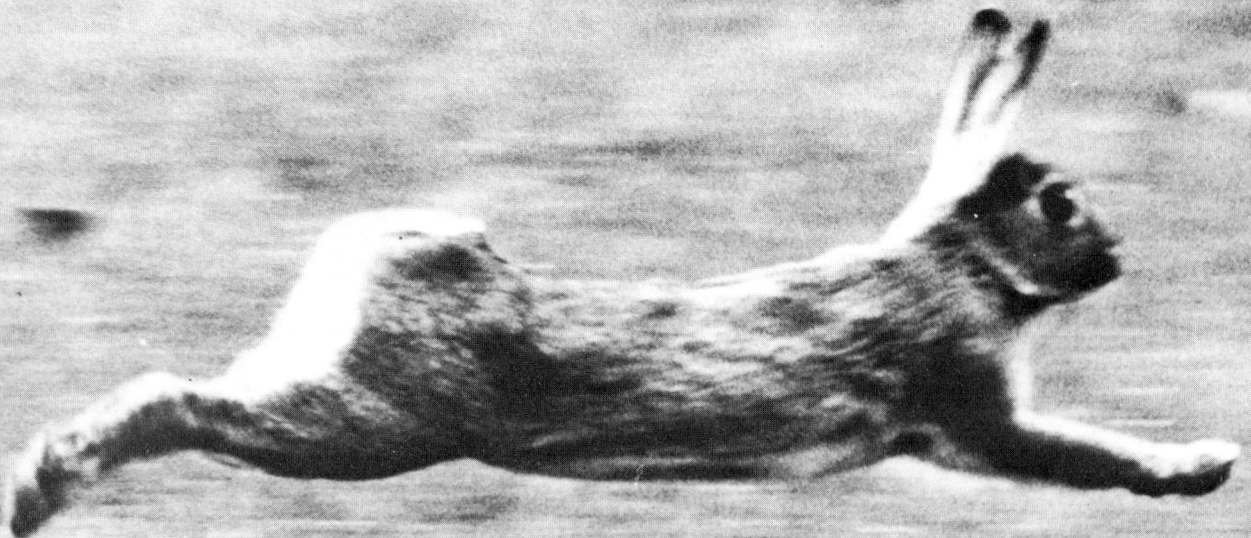

Like hares, rabbits have eyes which bulge out of the sides of their heads so that they can see behind as well as in front of them.

laws still refer to them as coneys.

When rabbits were taken from Britain to other countries overseas they needed far less time to make themselves at home. The enormous rabbit population of Australia is said to have been bred from 24 rabbits released in the State of Victoria in 1859. Within thirty years rabbits became a terrible pest, eating the pastures bare and making it impossible for sheep to live over thousands of square miles. The longest single fence in the world, of over a thousand miles, was put up to keep them out of

one Australian state, but the rabbits had found their way to the other side before it was finished. In the warm, dry climate the rabbits did not even bother to dig burrows but made their nests in scoops in the sand dunes, pressing on always into new territory.

Much the same happened in New Zealand, where rabbits first became established in about 1864. In the

There were so many rabbits in South Australia that farmers had "rabbit drives", like cattle drives, to round them up.

1930s over 13,000,000 skins were being exported from New Zealand every year. The damage done by the rabbits was, however, so great that, in spite of the profit from the trade in skins and meat, the New Zealand Government tried hard to kill them all off.

Rabbits were also introduced to Chile, in South America, where they soon became a serious pest.

Above: A beagle chases a cottontail. The cottontail dodges and swerves to confuse the dog and escape.
Left: A rabbit has a quick sniff at some bracken.

Faced with the damage done by rabbits, most countries where they are common have tried to get rid of them. Most books about rabbits contain chapters on how to catch and kill them.

In Britain rabbits were often caught in wire snares, set in the rabbits' tracks or runs, as with hares. Steel gin traps, which are now illegal, were also used. Many rabbits, too, were shot.

Ferrets were much used in catching rabbits. A ferret is a thin, active, flesh-eating animal of the weasel family.

63

It looks very like a stoat. Rabbit catchers put nets over all the holes in a warren and then let a ferret loose down one of the holes. The ferret hunts the rabbits through the underground tunnels and chases them out, to be caught in the nets.

Stoats and weasels, the near relations of the ferret, are two of the worst enemies of the wild rabbit. Stoats follow rabbits for hours, until the rabbit gives in and waits to be killed. It is said that they seem to hypnotise the rabbit. Both stoats and weasels enter the rabbit's burrows, especially the nesting burrows if they can find them, and kill the young. Foxes, dogs and badgers dig out young rabbits. Outdoors, hawks by day and owls by night pounce on rabbits, especially young ones. In countries where they live many snakes, too, will swallow any young rabbits they can find.

One of the reasons why rabbits became so numerous in Britain is that most of the larger animals, such as lynxes, wolves and eagles, which would prey on them, have all been killed. In Australia and New Zealand, too, the rabbits found few natural enemies. Weasels, foxes and mongooses were brought into these countries to deal with the hordes of rabbits, and in some cases these became pests themselves.

The rabbit problem in most countries was at last solved by a disease called *myxomatosis*. This is a disease caused, like the common cold in human beings, by a virus. Rabbits

The cottontail leaps and swoops through the snow.

Rabbits, of course, have many enemies. *Above:* A fox with a dead cottontail. *Below:* A buzzard feeds its young.

suffering from myxomatosis have swollen eyes, ears and other parts of the body. They become blind and deaf and eventually die. The disease is spread by the rabbit flea and by mosquitoes.

Myxomatosis was discovered in South America many years ago. In 1950 it was brought into Australia in an attempt to control the huge rabbit population. It proved so successful that in some parts of Australia 99% of the rabbits died. The Australians were pleased because the land which was formerly grazed only by rabbits could now be used by sheep, which produce meat and wool.

Two years later myxomatosis was brought into France for the same purpose. The disease spread rapidly over most of Europe, though it was not welcomed everywhere. The French had, as well as many wild rabbits, over 10,000,000 domestic breeding rabbits, kept for meat, and they did not want to see these all die from myxomatosis. Many of them did, however.

Nobody knows how myxomatosis came to Britain. Some people think it was brought over from France by birds or on the wheels of cars; some think it was introduced deliberately. Whatever the means, it appeared in 1953 and soon spread to almost every part of the country. Enormous numbers of rabbits died, and rabbits have been rather scarce ever since.

However, whenever a disease attacks a race of animals, there are always a few individuals which are immune.

A sign of danger: a rabbit shows its white scut and vanishes.

This happened with rabbits and myxomatosis. The surviving rabbits which were not affected by the disease went on breeding and so produced a race of rabbits which were immune. So the numbers of rabbits have been increasing again. The British Government, like the governments of other countries in which myxomatosis occurred, was anxious to keep rabbits under control and so made grants of money to kill off the survivors. In spite of everything, rabbits are managing to breed faster than they can be killed.

10: Friends and Relations

Other kinds of rabbits are to be found in most countries. America has the Cottontail, of which there are five different sorts. It also has the Marsh Rabbit, the Swamp Rabbit and several Pygmy Rabbits. Cottontails are rather smaller than European rabbits, though very similar in appearance. Pygmy rabbits are really small, weighing only about a pound. They live in the western states of America, where they often dig their burrows under sage bushes.

An American cottontail rabbit scuttles with long hind legs through the undergrowth.

Although quite common, American rabbits have never been as numerous as European rabbits, in Europe or Australia. This is chiefly because there are more flesh-eating animals in America to prey on them. Myxomatosis has not come to America because Cottontails are more or less immune to it, as are most of the rabbits found in South America.

In Africa the Bunyoro Rabbit, found in East Africa, is very like the European rabbit. The Riu-Kiu Rabbit of Japan has a thick, woolly coat, dark brown in colour, and tiny ears. Mexico has a pygmy rabbit found only on the slopes of two volcanoes and nowhere else in the world.

A desert cottontail is specially adapted to live where there is not much greenery and where it is very hot.

11 : Domestic Rabbits

Rabbits have long been domesticated. Some are kept for meat, and this has become a large industry in recent years. Some are kept for fur. Some are kept as pets.

Rabbit fanciers have bred many varieties of tame rabbits. They are of all colours, ranging from white and silver to black, orange and bluish. Among the commoner breeds are the following:

Chinchilla—large, silvery-grey rabbits.

Blue Beveren—large rabbits with slaty-grey fur.

Rex—have thick, dense, short fur, like velvet. Also known as Fox Rabbits. Generally rather small. There are several varieties, such as Havana Rex (which is dark brown), Lilac Rex, and Sable Rex.

Californian—a white rabbit with dark brown ears, paws and nose.

Dutch—a small rabbit, with short ears. Short fur, black and white.

Belgian Hare—a very large rabbit. Colour, chestnut. In spite of its name, it is a rabbit.

Angora—a white rabbit with a very long white coat of

A mixed collection of domestic rabbits, mother and young.

Out in the cold, a cottontail sits at the entrance to its burrow.

extremely fine hair, or wool, which can be plucked and
spun to make clothes.

Old English—a white rabbit, with a black stripe down the
back, rows of black spots along the side, and a black
mark, shaped like a butterfly, on its nose.

Flemish Giant—an enormous rabbit, grey in colour and
weighing up to 15 lb.

Himalayan—very like the Californian, but slimmer and
more elegant.

New Zealand White—a small, short-furred, white rabbit,
used for meat production on a large scale.

Rabbits kept as pets usually live in hutches, which should be large enough to give the animals plenty of space. If they can be given an outdoor run on a lawn as well, so much the better. They should be fed twice a day, on green material as well as some dry food, such as meal, pellets, hay or bread. They should always be provided with water. Female rabbits should be given a hutch of their own, with a dark inner compartment in which to make a nest. They should be supplied with plenty of hay or soft straw as litter.

Pet rabbits should *not* be lifted by the ears. One hand may hold the ears, to give control over the rabbit, but the weight of the animal should be taken on the other hand or arm, which is placed under its hind legs.

If you do all these things, and look after your rabbits carefully, your pets will give you much pleasure.

A fluffy family of white angora rabbits.

Glossary

BUCK. A male rabbit.

BURROW. A tunnel in the ground dug by rabbits.

CONEY. The original name of rabbits. The name *rabbit* was formerly used as a term of endearment, for young or pet rabbits, much as we now use the word *bunny*. Rabbits are still referred to as conies in legal documents.

DOE. A female rabbit or hare.

FORM. The place where a hare sits. It is usually a slight depression in the earth and is often concealed by grass or other plants.

GESTATION. The period between mating and the birth of a baby animal; the period during which the baby is carried in its mother's body.

GREGARIOUS. Sociable; animals which live in flocks or groups are called gregarious.

HUTCH. A box made to house tame rabbits.

IMMUNITY. Freedom from infection by the germs of a disease. Some rabbits are immune from infection by myxomatosis.

JACK. A male hare is known as a jack hare.

76

LEVERET. A young hare.

MOULT. The seasonal shedding of a coat of fur or hair.

MYXOMATOSIS. A deadly disease which affects rabbits.

NOCTURNAL. A nocturnal animal is one which is active at night.

POLYGAMOUS. A male animal with more than one wife. There is a distinction between a polygamous animal and a *promiscuous* one. The wives of a polygamous male mate with him and with no other. Promiscuous animals mate with whatever member of the opposite sex they happen to find. Rabbits are polygamous; hares are thought to be promiscuous.

PREY UPON. To hunt and kill another animal for food.

REFECTION. The peculiar arrangement whereby hares and rabbits eat their own pellets, thus giving themselves a second chance to digest their food.

RING-BARKING. When a tree has its bark eaten away, as by rabbits or hares, in a complete circle it is said to be ring-barked. The sap cannot rise, and so the tree dies.

RUNS. Tracks used regularly by rabbits and hares.

STOP. The nesting burrows of rabbits, so called because the mother rabbit stops the entrance with earth and refuse when leaving it, to conceal it from enemies.

TERRITORY. An area of land regarded by an animal as its own property. Animals will drive other animals of the same species away from their territory. Thus a female rabbit will chase away another female rabbit which

77

trespasses on her territory but will pay no attention to a different sort of animal, such as a cow or a hare.

VEGETARIAN. An animal which eats only plants.

WARREN. A maze of underground tunnels in which a colony of rabbits live.

Finding Out More

You should look for brown hares in open country. They may be seen running across fields or moors. Sometimes we may almost stumble over one as it sits in its form. If baby hares are found they should be left where they are. Their mother knows where they are.

Look for numbers of hares on airfields. Also look for assemblies of hares in March.

Alpine hares are to be seen on moors and mountains in Scotland. Some have been introduced to northern England and Wales.

Rabbits are found in more wooded country, and especially on farmland with plenty of hedges. They run back into the hedges, where their burrows are, when disturbed.

Tame rabbits may be seen in Children's Corners in almost every zoo. They may also be bought in every pet shop.

Books to read:–

H. V. Thompson & A. N. Worden, *The Rabbit*

H. Dyson, *Rabbits*

L. Harrison Matthews, *British Mammals*

Maurice Burton, *Systematic Dictionary of Mammals of the World*

Marion Nixon, *The Oxford Book of Vertebrates*

The Living World of Animals (Readers Digest Association)

Maxwell Knight, *Pets, Usual & Unusual*

Jeremy Lingard, *Zoo in the Garden*

M. J. Lawrence & R. W. Brown, *Mammals of Britain: their Tracks, Trails and Signs*

The Council for Nature, Zoological Gardens, Regent's Park, London, NW1 4RY, is a centre for information about animals in Britain.

Index

Picture Credits

The author and publishers thank the following for permission to reproduce copyright illustrations on the pages indicated: Ardea Photographics, *frontispiece*, 6, 14, 18, 30, 32–3; Frank W. Lane, 8, 10, 11, 12, 15, 17, 19, 22, 24, 28, 29, 38, 39, 41, 44, 45, 49, 51, 55, 65 (bottom), 66, 69, 75; Bruce Coleman Ltd, 9, 16, 20–1, 27, 34, 36, 37, 40, 42, 48, 52, 54, 58, 59, 62, 63, 65 (top), 70, 74; Pictorial Press Ltd, 26, 46, 72–3; Paul Popper Ltd, 50, 60–1; Natural History Photographic Agency, 56, 68.